The one thing that was missing from Hanukkah celebrations is a healthy helping of Cat Butts. But(t) not anymore! Meowzel!

Now you can have 8 days and nights of Cat Butts baking, eating latkes, spinning dreidels, collecting gelt, lighting the Meownorah and more.

Grab your coloring implements, a stack of latkes to snack on and let Cat Butt Hanukkah make this your best Hanukkah ever!

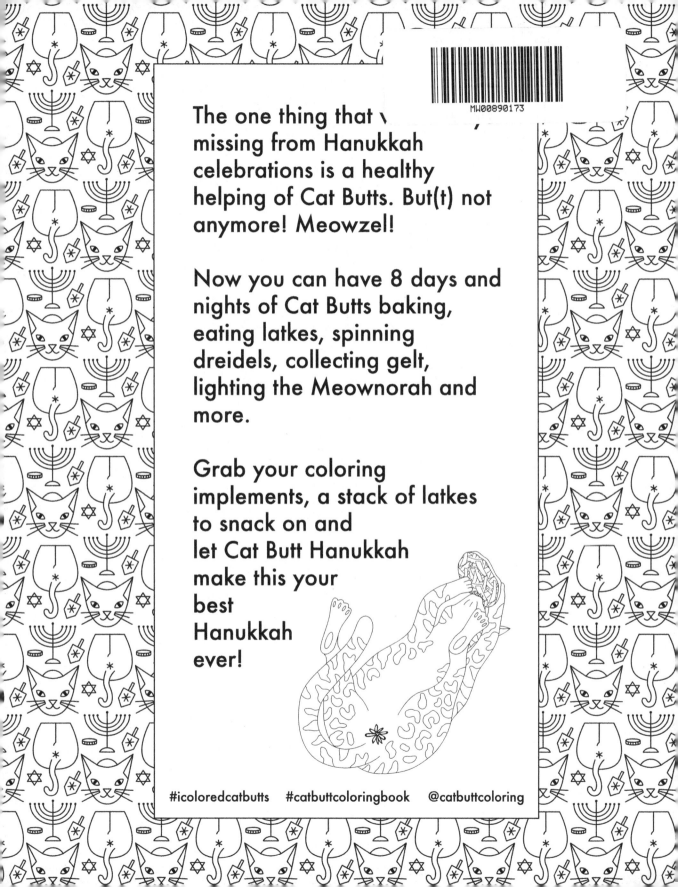

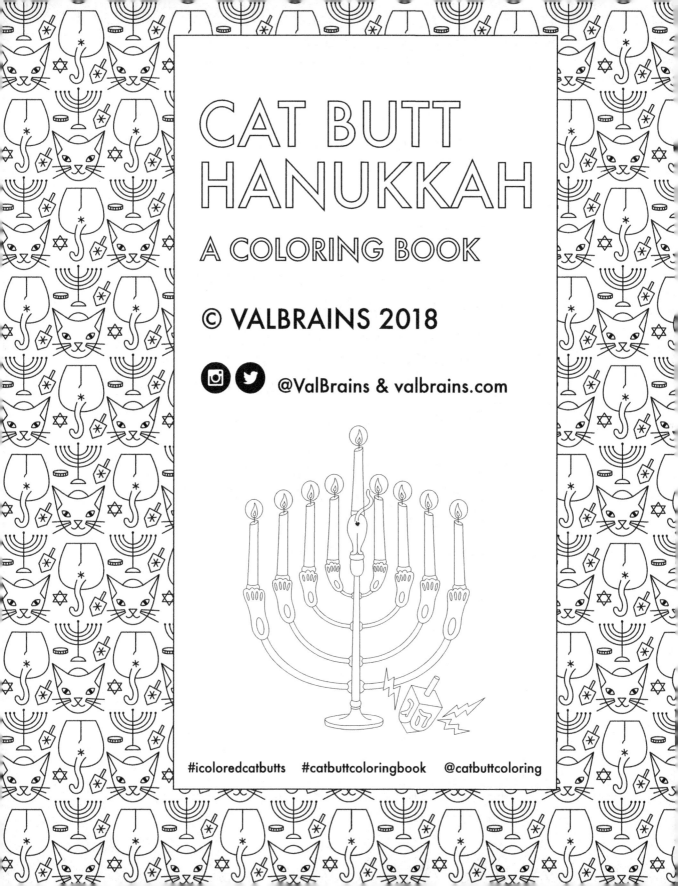

CAT BUTT HANUKKAH

A COLORING BOOK

© VALBRAINS 2018

@ValBrains & valbrains.com

#icoloredcatbutts   #catbuttcoloringbook   @catbuttcoloring

SUFGANIY-OOPS!

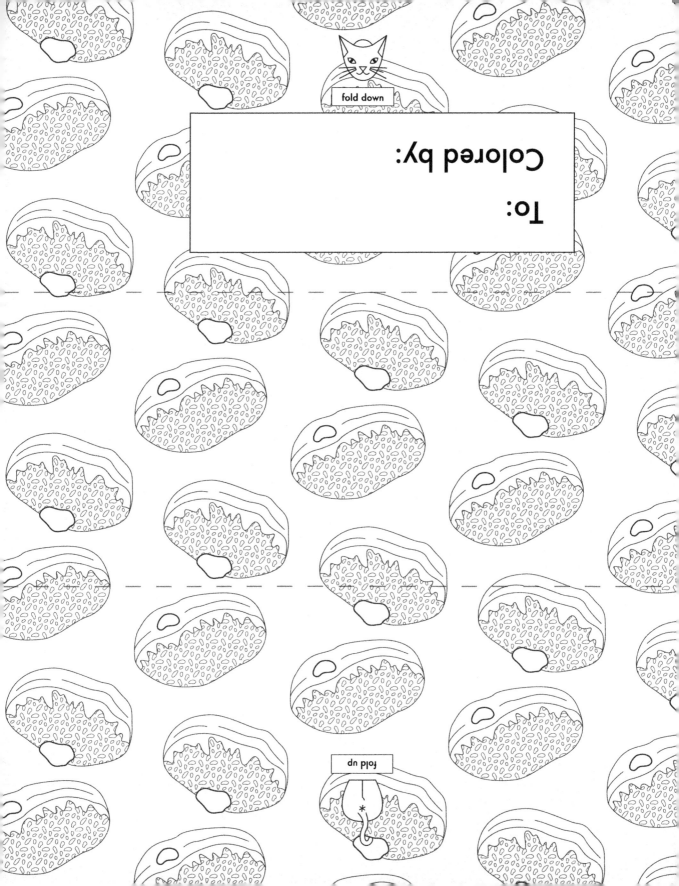

fold down

To:

Colored by:

fold up

HANUKKOOKIES

fold down

Colored by:

To:

fold up

LATKE LOVER

fold down

To:

Colored by:

fold up

MEOWNORAH

fold down

Colored by:

To:

fold up

GELT GETTER

fold down

To: Colored by:

fold up

8 NIGHTS OF PRESENTS!

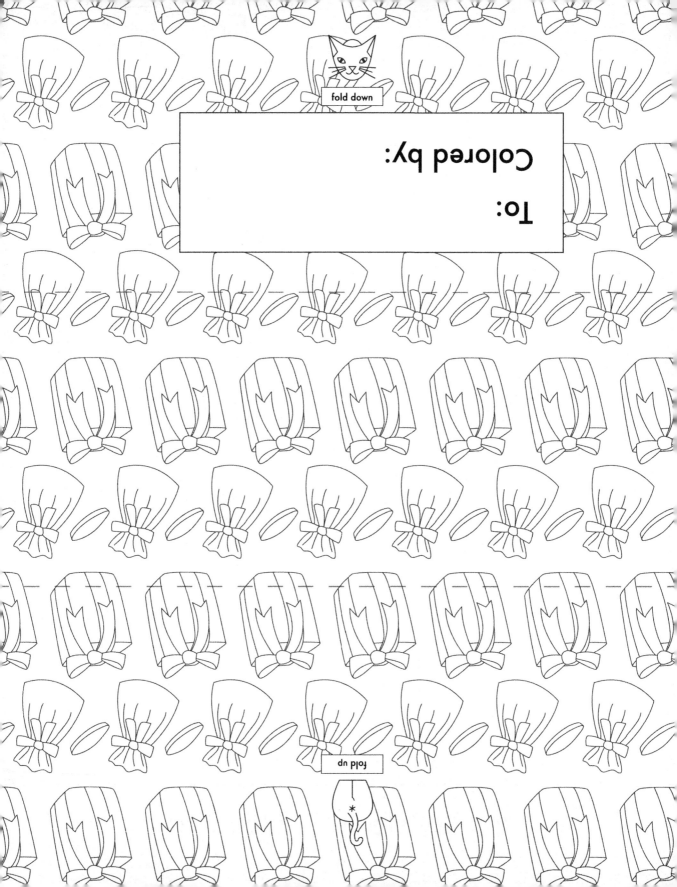

fold down

To:

Colored by:

fold up

OIL LAMP ENCOUNTER

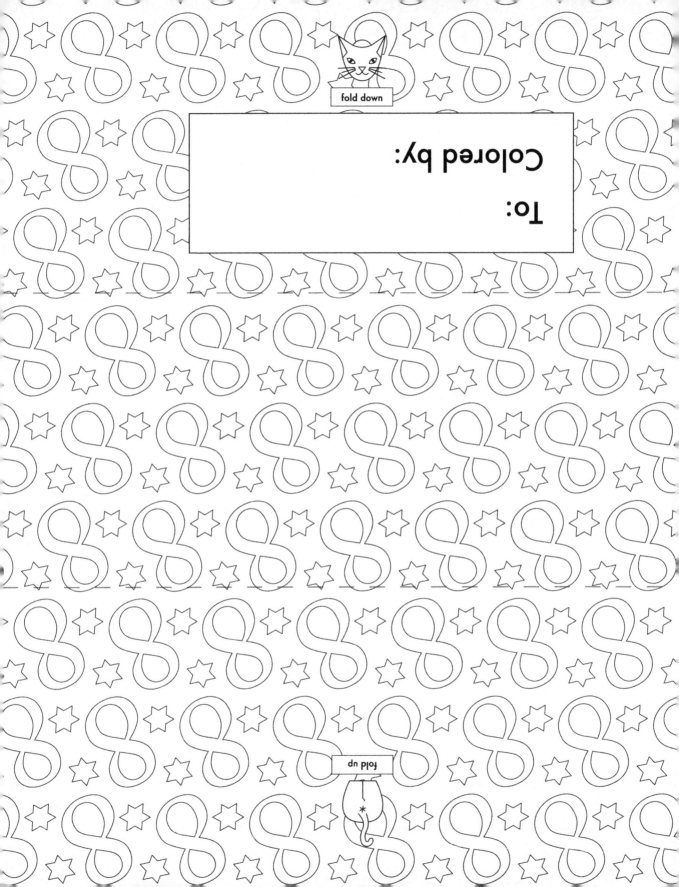

fold down

To:

Colored by:

fold up

GRATE EXPECTATIONS

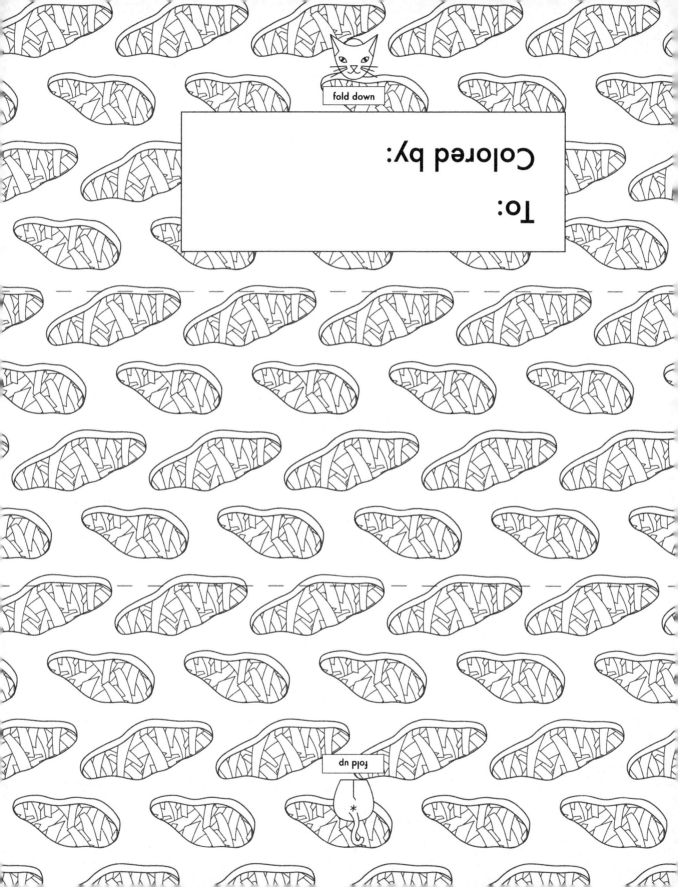

fold down

To:

Colored by:

fold up

DREIDEL, DREIDEL

fold down

To:

Colored by:

fold up

LATKE LOUNGING

fold down

Colored by:

To:

fold up

GOLDEN SURPRISE

fold down

To:

Colored by:

fold up

SHAMOEWSH

fold down

Colored by:

To:

fold up

CATTY HANUKKAH!

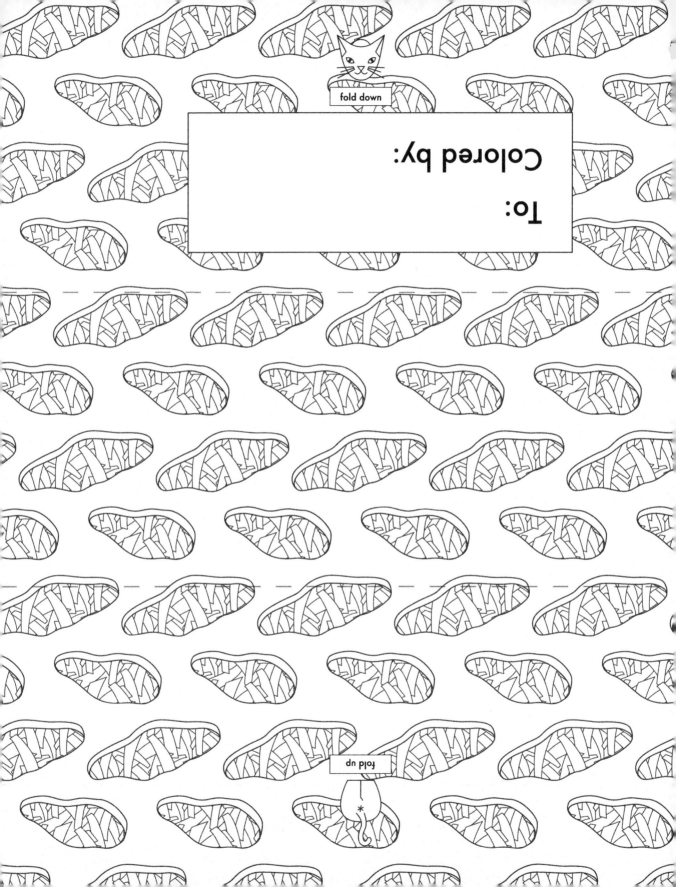

fold down

To: Colored by:

fold up

HANUKKAH VISION

fold down

Colored by:

To:

fold up

DREIDEL BLIZZARD

fold down

Colored by:

To:

fold up

8 BUTTS OF HANUKKAH

fold down

Colored by:

To:

fold up

SPELLING SPECULATION

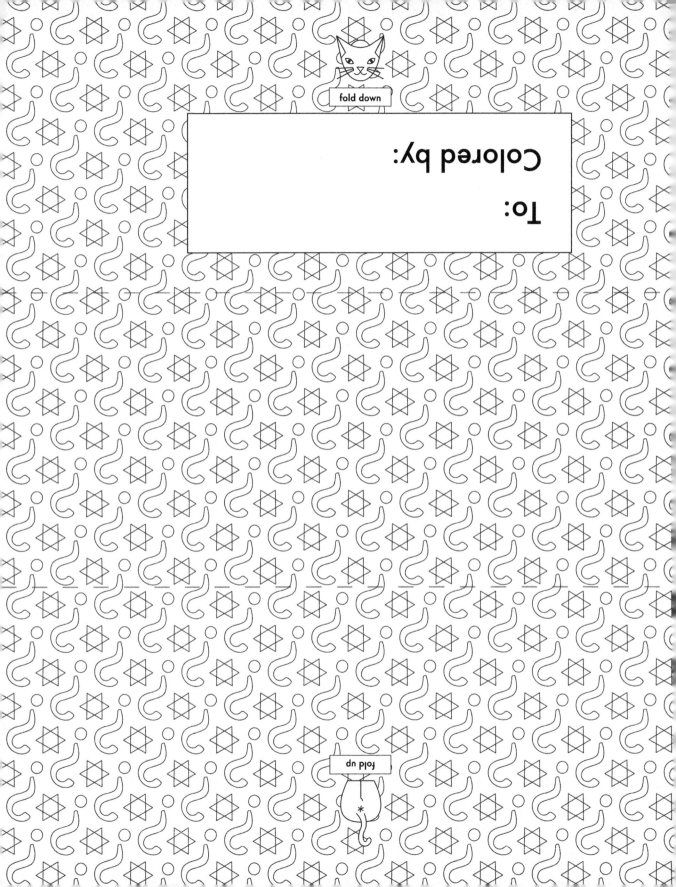

fold down

To:

Colored by:

fold up

I MADE IT OUT OF CLAY

fold down

To:

Colored by:

fold up

TORAH TUSH

fold down

To: _____

Colored by: _____

fold up

DREIDEL DANCING

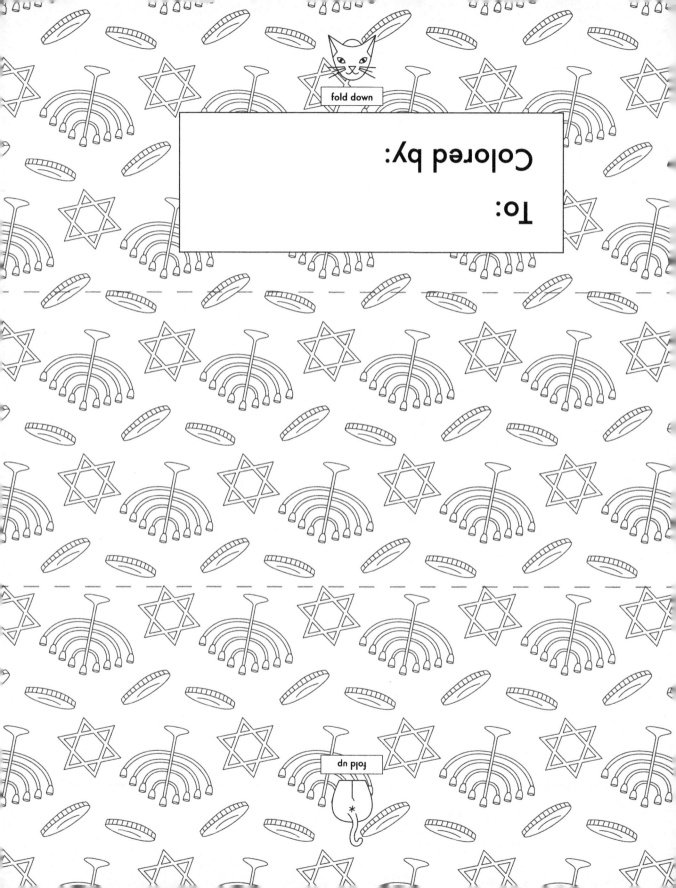

fold down

To: Colored by:

fold up

A
CAT BUTT HANUKKAH
HAIKU

Cat Butt Hanukkah
Is the festival of lights
Just with more cat butts

Thank you for coloring!

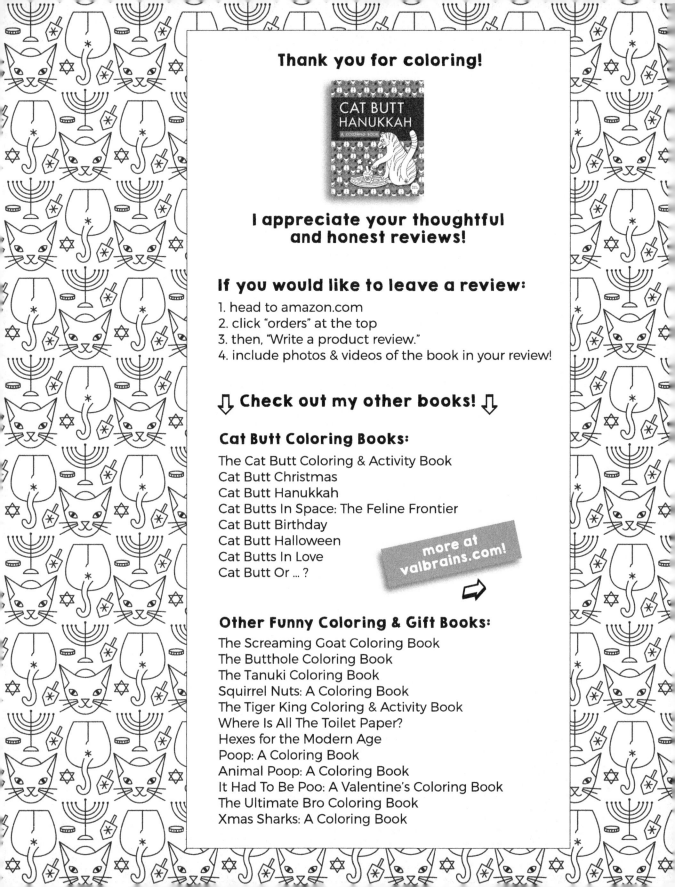

I appreciate your thoughtful and honest reviews!

If you would like to leave a review:

1. head to amazon.com
2. click "orders" at the top
3. then, "Write a product review."
4. include photos & videos of the book in your review!

⇩ Check out my other books! ⇩

Cat Butt Coloring Books:

The Cat Butt Coloring & Activity Book
Cat Butt Christmas
Cat Butt Hanukkah
Cat Butts In Space: The Feline Frontier
Cat Butt Birthday
Cat Butt Halloween
Cat Butts In Love
Cat Butt Or ... ?

more at valbrains.com! →

Other Funny Coloring & Gift Books:

The Screaming Goat Coloring Book
The Butthole Coloring Book
The Tanuki Coloring Book
Squirrel Nuts: A Coloring Book
The Tiger King Coloring & Activity Book
Where Is All The Toilet Paper?
Hexes for the Modern Age
Poop: A Coloring Book
Animal Poop: A Coloring Book
It Had To Be Poo: A Valentine's Coloring Book
The Ultimate Bro Coloring Book
Xmas Sharks: A Coloring Book

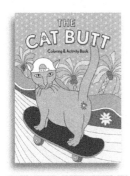

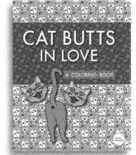

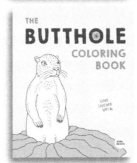

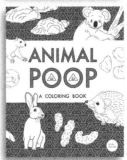

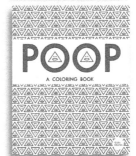

more at valbrains.com! ⇨

Made in United States
North Haven, CT
20 October 2021